Grief

&

Growth

A Part of Life

Dr. Tom Morris
Author of *Discuss Grief*

GrievingTeens Publishing

Third Publishing 2010 (with revisions and additions)

By
GrievingTeens™ Publishing
PO Box 14370
Palm Desert, CA 92255
Grievingteens@gmail.com

GrievingTeens.com
&
igriefresources.com

First Published in 2008 by YTC Press, Cambridge, UK
Former ISBN: 978-1-40920127-4

New ISBN: 978-0-557-15944-4

This Must Be Said!

The students that attended GreivingTeens™ grief groups from 1997-2010 @ Palm Desert High School, Desert Hot Springs High School, Cathedral City High School, and La Quinta High School were my greatest teachers. They are the ones who moved me to learn about their grief. They taught me through their losses that made this book possible. They allowed me to learn for they trusted me. Now I call many of them friends.

Contents

Preface

Life requires death as its conclusion. This is part of the human condition. Growth from death is only an option. Growth is a goal that can only be achieved with effort. Many people are "torn down" by grief and it sets them back. I have had family and friends that have never recovered from loss. Growing is a choice. Choose growth or choose life. The decision is only yours. The wise choice is growth.

I was spared any direct experience with funerals until I was twenty-three years old. Yes, there had been deaths in our family. My maternal grandfather and within months my grandmother died when I was eight, but they lived far away. My mother went back for one of the two funerals. I had neighbors and friends who died but attending their funerals never crossed my mind. Looking back, I know my parents were trying to protect me from death. Out of sight, out of mind was the prevailing attitude of the age. Even when my father's mother died I was unaware of the funeral. Finally, during seminary while serving as a student assistant pastor, I attended and conducted my first funeral.

Since then, I have lost many family members and friends through the years. I have come to understand much better what it is "to be acquainted with grief." Unexpectedly in 1994, I lost a friend in the ministry to AIDS, which was a terrible loss and shock. I realize that I may have been a "late starter" in dealing with death, but like almost every person, as I have gotten older, my awareness of death has grown. Sooner or later, death gets everyone's attention.

It was not that my life was loss-free in High School. It was just that I did not attend funerals. The greatest loss of my teens was not in death, although I had acquaintances at school that died. My loss, which crippled my life for several years internally, was the loss of my friends in moving from Denver, Colorado to Utica, New York at the age of 15 in the middle of my Sophomore year of high school. It took me at least a year to decide to grow from the experience. That decision has affected my life and ministry since.

Ten years ago, a good friend asked me to speak to his health classes on Death and Dying, after his own parents had recently died. He admitted that though the subject of death was part of the curriculum, he simply couldn't imagine handling the discussion. Being too painful, he had avoided the subject of death. I told him, "Yes, I'll speak to your class," and called a funeral home to borrow a casket—a prop for the front of the room to help set the stage. I spoke for 45 minutes about death. For most students it was their first extended discussion of the subject. They had never discussed it at home. As they talked about death, their unresolved issues about mortality and grief came to the surface. This book is the result of that invitation to speak and the needs it uncovered.

I started facilitating grief groups in the spring of the 1997-98
school year. Since then, we have held two to four groups each year.
This book contains what I have learned through my experience within these teen groups. I have also completed a Doctoral program at Trinity Evangelical Divinity School in Deerfield, Illinois. While at Trinity, I was encouraged to develop my ministry to teens, which I named, Grieving Teens™. For more information go to **grievingteens.com**

It has brought richness and meaning in my life to witness young people, broken in grief, hurting, and expressing bitterness, recover and grow to be stronger people with the help of God's grace. I'm proud of them. Given the right tools, insights, and time, they have grown through grief. The point is for them to find the Resurrection and the Life. I pray this will be true for you as well.

Life always includes its share of losses and good-byes. Coping and growing in and through change and loss is part of the process of life here on earth. I have found that the God of all comfort will comfort you if you ask for His help and comfort.

It is my hope and prayer that this book and others will be a guide to you on your journey through life. The journey begins with the ten practical steps you can take in response to grief and loss. Many will not be easy. But they will get you moving in the right direction. Remember, there is absolutely nothing you are going through, in which God doesn't know about. Remember that God knows you. And remember He wants you to know Him. I pray that you will trust the Author of Life with your life.

Tom Morris

2010

Ten Steps
When You Face Grief or Loss...

1. The news of a loss will leave your life shaken and your feelings numb and in shock. Whether it is a death, divorce, break-up of a close friendship or relationship, loss of a job, a major move, or when a combination of more than one loss strikes, stop and ask God to help you, your family and friends. Pray to the God of all comfort, to comfort you.

2. Give yourself time to face the reality of whatever has happened. Face it squarely. Some can do this in hours. For others it takes weeks, or months. Keep your head out of the sand. Face the truth. Live in the Light.

3. Call your family and friends and ask for their support in this time. You need them and you need their prayers and encouragement. You will not need lectures but friends and family that will be there for you. You need people who care about you.

4. Your emotions may overwhelm you like a rising tide. Allow yourself the freedom to feel and face the reality of your feelings. Talk to others who care and who will seek to understand. Share with people you trust. You need people who will not try to fix you, but just listen.

5. Do not think that because you are a good person, religious or even a Christian you will get through grief painlessly. God will be with you but you may take a journey through the valley of the shadow of death. Death will test and deepen your faith. Faith in the *end* stands firm through tests.

6. The death or loss you have experienced is not a surprise to God. He knows everything. He does not cause death. People and their sin cause pain and death. God uses pain in loss as everything else for good.

7. Contact your church or local community programs to find out if they offer grief support groups. Buy a copy of A Grief Observed by C. S. Lewis and walk through grief with a wise fellow *traveler*.

8. Grief can be a confusing time, and many people find that journaling helps them sort through memories and preserve valuable insights from their experience. Keep a list of your feelings—identify anger, doubt, joy, and name them in your records. Especially make a list of your fears. Create a record of your hopes. Also, make a list of your personal assets: physical,

spiritual, social, and emotional.

9. Expect grief to take work and effort. Working through grief is not just a matter of allowing time to pass. You will have to accept the loss and work through the grief by facing and dealing with your emotions and thoughts. (This is further explained in the first chapter).

10. Grief is not like a scheduled event. Do not think life will go on as it did before. You will have to focus time and thought on your loss. It will take time, but it has its own timetable. For some it takes years, while for others it takes less time. Be patient with yourself. Allow yourself the time needed. Do not try to return to *normal life* and expect that grief will then be over. Work through the grief. Busyness does not make grief go away; it merely delays or puts off the work.

Why is it that when we are in pain we try to deny the obvious? This does not work. The following attempts to make this point. Not that I, or any of you have ever been in a room with a rhino. Stop and imagine…

Big Black Rhino

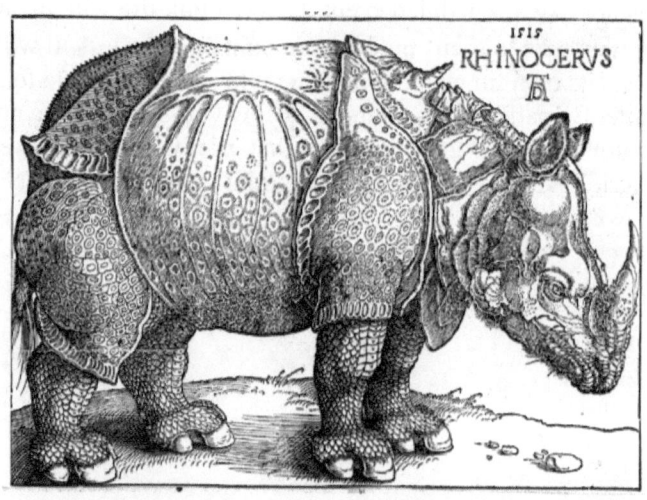

There is a big black rhino breathing in the room.
It's a huge snorting and impossible to avoid beast.
We gingerly move around the rhino - as if it were not there.
We say things like, "how are things?" We respond with "sweet"
Or "awesome" but we know the black rhino is there.
It snorts, it stares. And, life is not sweet.

There is a big black rhino breathing in the room.
Even though the black rhino blocks the doors and windows
we try to look out and talk about the weather,
the next game, work, or the upcoming movie.
We will speak of anything but the black rhino in the room.

There is a big black rhino breathing in the room.
Everyone sees it, hears it, and feels its hoofs pound the floor.
But, there is no way to approach the door.
We feel trapped, afraid, and angry.

The black rhino fills our thoughts but we do not speak of him.
Inside we ache but we don't show the inner quake.
There is a big black rhino breathing in the room.

We want others to mention or speak the name
behind the rhino's presence.
The ones we have lost to death, divorce or other losses.
No one speaks the names for fear of the black rhino.

The black rhino controls all in the room.
There was a big black rhino breathing in the room.
Then radical names were spoken behind the black rhino.
The names were spoken of the missing. With those names the fear and
anger slowly died.
The black rhino turned and lumbered out of the door.
In months, the fear of the black rhino returning melted away.

There was a big black rhino breathing in the room.
Let's keep talking about him.
I need to talk about the black rhino to keep it out of the room.
When another black rhino approaches I'll know what to do.
Until then I will need to talk and have others listen to me.
Help me keep the black rhino out of my room.
Encourage me to talk for if I don't I'll live alone in a room
with a black rhino.

T.L. Morris 2006

1
Our Human Situation...

Death is the last part of life as we now know it. Very few of us give much thought to death before it invades and overruns our lives. When it wins, nothing else seems to matter for a while. Death rips someone from us. One moment that person is here; the next, they are gone. We may not have any idea where—we just know they are not longer here with us.

Our own lives suddenly feel even briefer than imagined with the onset of terminal illness or sudden death. We are rudely reminded of our own mortality. We like to think of life as long, but for some it is short. All of us must come to grips with death.

It is difficult for those who lose loved ones early. We don't want to die, but longevity includes the prolonging of pain. Even if we live to be 100, that achievement will be darkened because everyone we loved will most likely have died while we remain alive we will feel increasingly alone.

Death brings with it a harsh companion we call grief. Grief is the wound death inflicts when it takes life. Grief is the tolling of the bells.

For Whom the Bell Tolls
John Donne

No man is an island,
Entire of itself.
Each is a piece of the continent,
A part of the main.
If a clod be washed away by the sea,
Europe is the less.
As well as if a promontory were.
As well as if a manner of thine own
Or of thine friend's were.
Each man's death diminishes me,
For I am involved in mankind.
Therefore, send not to know
For whom the bell tolls,
It tolls for thee.

The dead can't hear the bells – we do. Sometimes they sound distant, but often it feels like we're standing in the bell tower and the ringing is an emotional and physical shuddering of our souls. The vibrations go right through us. We wonder if they will ever stop. We ponder how we can go on. And we shake our heads in instinctive disbelief that anything good could come out of all this pain.

Growing through grief is not automatic. Grief is not like the effect of gravity on Earth where the shoe always drops. What you do and do not do will affect the lasting results of your loss. Countless people have fallen apart as a response to a major loss and their subsequent grief. Others have taken all the pain and meaning of their loss and gradually developed something amazing that recognizes the place of suffering in life. This is not so called "closure" (trying to seal up grief so it stops hurting). Nor is it "coping" (simply enduring grief in the hopes that it will wear out before we do). This is growth (allowing something terrible to have both its negative as well as positive effect in our lives). Growth is the option I hope you will choose.

Death provokes all of us to seriously consider what lies beyond this life. For many people, the death of someone close is also the first time they begin to treat life and God seriously. Death makes most people stop ignoring God or ignoring the possibility of God. They may rage at God or weep in His presence or groan for help. But they stop treating Him as if He doesn't exist. Death slaps an atheist across the face with the fact that his unbelief has no answer for death.

I'm writing this to those who are at least ready to consider God on His terms. If you are very angry with Him, He doesn't mind. The Bible is full of people who were angry at God and He loved them anyway. He loves you too, even if right at this moment you would violently slap His hand away if He tried to touch you. He's not offended by your anger—

He knows all about it. And when you're ready, He will help you pick up the pieces and keep growing.

You see, God wants those who know Him to grow, to become more like Christ. This is His goal for us. No matter what happens, good or ill, this is His purpose for you and me, if you know Him, to become like Christ -- perfect. One of my goals in this book is to help you understand what this means and apply it to the grief that fills your life. As with any trial in life, we can either grow through it and be strengthened in time, or it can damage and set us back. What will you choose? Do you know what God wants for you? With grief, which affects all of your life (emotionally, socially, and spiritually) you will either grow or become lost in your journey of life. If you become lost, your condition can affect even your physical health. A human is an integrated whole; the spirit, the mind and the body affect one another. In turn, our wellbeing influences other aspects of our life.

I vividly remember a girl who lived out the issues I've just described. Crystal regrouped internally after her parents' divorce and tried to cope. Late one night her father came to her room to tell her, in tears, that her mom had been shot and killed at a party. The TV blared the news of her mother's violent death across the airwaves. It seemed that the world had closed around her and no other news was reported that day, except the death of her mother. It was also a front-page story in the local paper. At school, everyone whispered behind her back but never talked directly to her. She spent hours crying and confused. To make matters worse, her father wept, screamed, and drank until the booze numbed him to sleep. He anesthetized the pain from his life with alcohol and drugs. Crystal and her three younger sisters were angry and afraid for themselves and their father.

This had gone on for nine months when I first met Crystal. She and six other young people wanted help in dealing with the pain of their individual losses. We began a journey through grief together. In the chapters that follow, you will read about some of the issues we worked through as a group. Perhaps this book can help you to work through some of your issues as well.

Chances are you are reading this book due to someone's death. Maybe someone gave it to you, or just left it on the counter. They may not have known what to say, but sensed that you were in pain due to your loss. This book seeks to help you in your own personal situation and guide you back to a sense of normality in your life. Questions surface when we get our heads above the shock of the news that someone we knew and/or loved has died.

Personal Growth and Discussion Questions:

1. Can you look yourself in the mirror and say too yourself, "I am going to die someday?"
2. What fears do you have?
3. How have you coped with your fear?
4. Do you think shyness has to do with fear why? Or why not?
5. What could happen in your life if the fears fade or disappear from your life?

2
This Can't Be Happening to Me!

"Mac's eyes shot open. The silence of the darkened living room covered him like a shroud. He wiped the sweat from his forehead.

If only.
He sat on the couch and rubbed his face, forcing reality into his pores. It had been nine months since he had come home to a house full of death and pain. Still, grief and guilt were all-consuming.
Debilitating. He found himself daydreaming a lot these days. It was an escape, a way to snatch moments of time where he could try to change what had happened, make it all go away.
Help me, God! I don't want to hurt anymore.
Show me how to move on. The guilt was overwhelming: guilt for not being home, guilt for believing that such evil would never dare touch his world, guilt for living on without her.

If only..."

These words, taken from the opening scene of a novel called,
Time Lottery by Nancy Moser, plunge us into the raw emotions of grief.
However as the saying goes, "Life is truer than fiction."
Words, and scenes, similar to the one involving the fictional character,
Mac, play out in real life every day.

Death happens! And it often strikes unexpectedly, like a bolt of lightning in a
clear blue sky. Accidents, floods, earthquakes, hurricanes, fire, war, and
suicide take their daily harvest of lives. Death can also take seemingly
healthy people in an instant. Autopsies reveal hidden time bombs like
aneurisms, embolisms, and blood clots that kill the unsuspecting. A person
may even die while asleep for no apparent reason.

When death is sudden, it has a devastating impact on the lives of those who
remain. Some know for months or years that death is stalking their lives,
while others are blind-sided. For young people in today's world, unexpected
deaths can be the result of reckless driving, out-of-control lifestyles, terrorist
attacks, school shootings, or gang violence. Grief, resulting from these types
of death, can be troublesome for young people for many years. Their
struggles can include problems such as: bad dreams, eating disorders, and a
lack of concentration in school.

These can affect home life, friendships and grades. They can lead to loss of
interest in normal daily activities or over-activity (trying to block out the
pain). Other symptoms of "undercover grief" may emotional distance or
wanting to be left alone, drug and/or alcohol abuse, anger issues, risk taking
behaviors (i.e. riding motorcycles or driving vehicles too fast),
anti-social behavior (such as bullying or even criminal behavior),
promiscuity, excessive concern or worry about health issues, pain and deep
sadness at the memory of the deceased, possibly leading to depression, or
worse, thoughts of or attempts at suicide. Buried or ignored grief doesn't die;
it simply finds expression through often self-destructive channels.

When death is sudden, a daze of unreality sets in called denial.
The shock of unexpected death can last hours, if not days and months.
It is common for people who experience sudden death to have nightmares, or
feelings of unrealistic guilt. They say to themselves, "if only..." as if there
was something they could have done to prevent the loss. That was Mac's
struggle in the opening vignette. Real guilt sometimes stems from
remembered words that were spoken in haste or anger to the person or
persons lost in death. In addition to guilt, there is a whole cluster of
emotions that go with that haunting sense of responsibility. Among these are

sadness, anger, frustration, fear and anxiety that ebb and flow when someone has experienced a loss.

If death is not sudden but expected, there is still shock at the realization that in two years or six months a loved one will die. Anticipatory grief occurs when the end is expected. Sometimes this gives time to adjust, while at other times it just allows for more pain.

Terminal diagnoses can spark wild hopes of a last minute miracle that can deepen the impact when death comes. When the anticipatory grief goes on and on, resentment can develop. This resentment then can lead to guilt for resenting your loved one's long illness. The process of death in a debilitating illness, like Alzheimer's, often leads to these feelings that seem so selfish. People who watch loved ones die in pain are often torn between their desire for life and their desire for an end to the pain.

Although Kübler-Ross' research and findings represented a milestone at the time of her publication, her works appear less than adequate now. Grief, as a process, (whether it comes in stages, phases, or tasks) is a matter of perspective that affects the whole person (physically, emotionally, socially, and spiritually) and is a response to loss. This book is based on a view of grief that identifies grief-phases that have a task component for the griever. This means that you have a responsibility to work through your grief. You can carry out responsive tasks that will engage your life in dealing with the loss you have experienced. These tasks have been taken from J. William Worden's *Grief Counseling and Grief Therapy*. The tasks are as follows:

Task I: Accept the Loss as Real

This means to move from shock and denial of death to mentally acknowledging that the death was real. Viewing the body of the dead loved one and attending the funeral will help in this first task.
Expressing what we will miss about that person and talking about them can also help. Friends often mistakenly avoid mentioning the dead person's name to avoid causing pain but actually create the vague suspicion in the one grieving that the world has already moved on and they are the only ones who still remember.

Task II: Work Through the Pain of Grief

Pain, hurt, anger, depression, and loneliness are some of the side effects of grief. Some or all of these appear constantly or intermittently as the previous

task takes effect. Give yourself permission to feel and work through the pain of grief. Trying to hold it in and suppress it will not help you or others. Remember, for some, it may take weeks or months, while for others, months or years. There is no set pattern or timeline.
Everyone's grief is as unique as the person who is dealing with it.

Task III: Adjust to a World Without the Deceased or Lost

External Adjustments
Adjusting to a loss is much broader than you might think or could imagine. What is an *external adjustment*? Learning to come home to an empty house can be an external adjustment. Coping with not being able to call your friend or relative when the urge arises, or being used to calling out to someone from the next room, are others. We have developed many habits involving our loved ones, things we take for granted, and when they are gone these external things are hard to change. An empty chair at the table or a missing voice in the conversation is an unexpected reminder of the loss and a new order of life. Other external adjustments may involve Dad bringing home the paycheck to pay the bills. At your Dad's death, there might be a change in income, which can mean that you will move to a cheaper place to live. And at the same time, you might have to make new friends.

Internal Adjustments
An *internal adjustment* usually involves your parent or best friend, as your primary emotional support. If they die, you will have to adjust your problem solving routine and your circle of intimacy to relate to a world without their emotional support. You will discover habitual expectations that will have to be changed. Your automatic mental picture of the next family gathering or a traditional event in which that person has always participated will have to lose their face in the portrait of your mind.

Spiritual Adjustments
When death occurs, especially an unexpected death, it usually makes us rethink our values and beliefs. A *spiritual adjustment* will often take place somewhere in the grief process. If we have a strong, practicing faith, it can prove to be our foundation and deepen. Our spiritual foundation is usually tested when dealing with death. But people often discover their spiritual poverty when it comes to dealing with death. It can awaken a renewed longing to know God. They come to realize that they do not have any

answers to the questions the death of a loved one evokes.

Task IV: Emotionally Place the Person or Relationship(s) in a new place & Move on With Life

You still love and care for the person who has died, but in a different way. And while life continues, it continues with a feeling of emptiness in your heart as you do continue living. C.S. Lewis spoke of losing a person being like having a hole in your heart. That hole in your heart, cannot be replaced by anyone else. This step is learning to cope with that hole. Even after death -- your parents will always be your parents.

Personal Growth and Discussion Questions:

1. Was your loss sudden or expected?
2. If you have experienced both kind(s) of loss, how did the losses differ for you?
3. If it your loss was sudden, how would you describe any experiences of guilt or emotional pain you felt due to the suddenness of the loss?
4. If you knew a loved one was going to die soon, in what ways did the extra time allow you time to grieve? How did the added time make death hard?
5. If it was an expected death, how were you able to say good-bye?
6. If it there has been a sudden death, what would you have wanted to say to the person who died?

Suggested Session Activities:

1. Have participants complete the form: "My Story."
2. Put a paper "mural memorial" on the wall and write or draw a message, symbol or sketch for the person you have lost.
3. Keep a journal or memory book in which to write and/or draw thoughts and feelings. C. S. Lewis entitled his, *A Grief Observed*.
4. Write a poem, eulogy, or song and share it with the group or special friends when appropriate.
5. Go on a field trip to a cemetery. Include times for quiet observation and

group interaction.

6. Launch balloons (biodegradable ones) after writing messages to the person(s) who died.

My Story:

The person who died in my life is...

The cause of death was..

I found out about the death when...

After death, I believe my loved one is..................................

My first feeling was ....because........................

....

Now I feel........................because...................................

....

What makes me most angry is..

I worry about........................because...............................

The hardest thing about school/work is.................................

Because...

My friends are..

The adults in my life tell me...

....

What helps me most is..

....

What helps me the least is...

3
What We Learn About Loss

Until I was 22 years of age, I had only seen funerals on TV and
in movies. I was a Youth Pastor and the Senior Pastor was out of town. I had
just returned from Summer Camp, in August of 1975, and the Church
secretary told me the Pastor wanted me to, "do a funeral." Why had I never
been to a funeral? My next thought was, "I hope it is not an open casket!"

I spoke with the family members and prayed with them. My hope in the
Gospel was my only preparation. My neighbor had died, my grand parents
had died, and even friends died while I was in Middle
School. Yet, this was my first funeral. Why had I been shielded from death
by never attending a funeral? JFK's funeral was the one that stuck in my
mind (along with Sir Winston Churchill's). An ordinary funeral is similar but
quite different.

My parents thought, and the prevailing culture's thinking was, that it was too
much for children to have to face death. So, let them live without death, or its
pain, if at all possible. My perspective on life was not balanced. How could it
be without the negative—death? Life is not only made up of newborn

puppies. Real life has death as well—dead dogs, dead cats, gold fish, etc.

In the course of life we learn many things. We learn how to get what we want. We learn how to please the teacher and get good grades, or we learn how to cheat the system. There is good and bad learning. We receive education about sports, history, math, science, and English. We learn how to acquire things by working or earning money to get what we want or need. We can learn about almost anything, except how to lose a friend or a parent or spouse. Life is a mixture of losses and gains, yet few have read a book on grief before experiencing it. Most of the time we are ill prepared to deal with loss. Why is this?

Years ago, my sister and brother-in-law lost their house and most of their personal belongings in a fire. The once beautiful, two-story home on a lake in Michigan was now a smoldering pile of soot and ash. The useful home was now useless debris. They experienced a waiting period until the insurance company got into gear. Friends and neighbors took care of their needs in the meantime. Their home was covered by "replacement cost insurance." This meant, in reality, that for months they were buying everything new. The old stereo was now a new and much improved model. The former drawer of used sox was now a drawer of new sox. The house was rebuilt, larger and with all the features they had wished they had the first time. Yes some things were lost but most material things were replaced.

We often times handle human loss the same way we handle the loss of possessions. If we lose a watch, we buy another. If something is stolen, insurance, Mom and Dad, or the grand parents will replace the lost item with a new and, perhaps, better one.

What did your parents do if you lost a pet? Almost everyone can remember having a pet when he/she was a child: a fish, puppy, turtle, or even a bird. At least one died every year, if not more often, in my home. I can remember several fish that died over night. I would get up and look at the fish bowl and see the new guppy dead and floating on the surface of the water. At the time, I was upset. My fish died! The money I had earned doing chores had been spent on my fish and their care, and now, the way I saw it, everything was gone—money and fish!

Your parents or grandparents probably said something like,
"It's ok. Do not feel bad…fish die. But we can go to the store and get another one soon." Now, as a parent, I understand that parents do not want to see their children in pain. A parent does not want to feel helpless. Doing something makes us feel better. It gets the child to stop crying and keeps the adult from feeling helpless. When we do this to others we try to fix the

situation and communicate the thought, as parents or grandparents frequently do, "Do not feel bad. We'll get you another of whatever you lost." We are telling the child not to feel the pain of loss, and that the fish can be easily replaced.

For many, this works well for years. When something is lost, it is replaced in a timely way to remove as much adjustment to loss as possible and minimize emotional response – the pain of loss.
A young person that has been protected from the affects of loss, will most likely, eventually, get into a friendship (male or female). That relationship will be very important to them emotionally. When people or their connection changes the relationship will likely break up on the rocks of life. The young person's life will fall apart for a few hours, days, or weeks. Friendship, which is lost, cannot simply be replaced.

Some try to use the "replacement" method, which worked in childhood, which was to quickly replace the relationship with another in order to cope with the loss. Some continue this tactic into adulthood, resulting in great pain. If you lose, then replace that which is lost. Do not let yourself feel bad. Rebound! Quickly finding a replacement is a tempting tactic that doesn't work.

Even more to the point, what about the loss of a Mom or Dad, or a tragic accident that takes away a loved one we cannot live without? Our response reveals we are ill prepared for what turns out to be unavoidable. We expect that somehow these relationships will be replaced. We assume something or someone will show up to take away the awful, relentless pain. But people cannot be replaced, for we are all unique, one-of-a-kind. When we loose a person, there will always be a hole or a missing piece in our lives. In time, our lives may feel bullet riddled with countless holes from a lifetime of losses. Not only that, but we cannot just "get over" a loss. We will feel helpless. Others will feel helpless to help, but that is the nature of real loss.

There is an essential loneliness in grief, which is part of the modern *global village* experience: "Laugh and the whole world laughs with you, cry and you cry alone." This poly-cultural attitude shows us that people are uncomfortable with expressions of emotion, and that when we do emote, we should be alone. Unfortunately, crying is often associated with shame.

Many of my older friends, including my family, have lived by this code concerning the showing of certain emotions. Men are not to be seen (by their families) in tears—ever. Only weak women cry in public. Some people feel they cannot show their emotion; they must remain strong for others. "Real men cry," I tell the students I work with. Sometimes, the world would like us to go to our rooms and cry alone. However, we need the comfort of others we trust in times of tears.

Personal Growth and Discussion Questions:

1. As you were growing up, how were you "trained" to handle grief?
2. How were loss and pain handled in your family? Was it ok to express grief? What was acceptable and what was unacceptable?
3. Was replacement the way pet and possession losses were handled in your life?
4. How do you want to prepare your child or students for life's painful circumstances?
5. Is it permissible to show emotion in front of others in your family? Why or why not?
6. How do you feel about letting others know or see you cry?
7. In what ways could you express your grief in front of others?
8. How do you handle grief in the lives of others?

4

Facing Death

Wham, bang – you are hit with the unexpected. Your mother has been diagnosed with the dreaded C word – Cancer. Your friend has been killed in a car crash. Your parents are getting a divorce and one of them is moving away. You feel like you've been sucker punched-dazed. At first, your head is spinning with disbelief.

The blaring unfairness echoes through your mind. Life is not supposed to be this way, you think to yourself. The longer we live, however, the more likely we are to find ourselves playing roles in dramatic scenes for which we have not prepared:

• You can call a friend's parents for his number, because it is no longer listed in the phonebook. The working assumption is, that he has moved. They tell you that, during the six months before, when you were out of touch, he had gone to the dentist and found that there was a malignant growth on his tongue. You were supposed to go camping during the summer, but he never called. He died!

• You can pick up the newspaper, and read that another friend has just died, and that the funeral is tomorrow.

• Your best friend's life and yours have traveled a parallel journey that seemed destined for endless adventures, but it can come to an end. You played sports together, went on double dates together, decided to attend college together, and even planned to go into business together. And then, a car crash brings this life and future plans to an end.

As the years go by, we learn to recognize death by its stark cold shadow moving back and forth across our lives.

How do we face death? Death affects our whole person. Like a jewel, man has more than one facet; a person has physical, mental, social, and spiritual facets. Death touches each of these areas. We first learn to face death in and through the deaths of others – grandparents, neighbors, friends, and family. The other way we learn to face death is when we find that our own lives may be cut short due to disease. The stark reality is that, one way or another, we will learn to face the fact people do die.

The people we know who die will be physically absent from our life. Even if we are present at the moment of their deaths, we are struck by the difference. Something undeniable is suddenly missing from the body in which they lived. They are gone. Mentally and emotionally, we may feel alone, abandoned, and empty. We will miss them. Our social networks that included that person will be changes because he or she is missing. Our spirituality will be tested by questions that reveal beliefs about death and life. If we have not thought about life and death, our personal loss may plunge us into a search for meaning. Suddenly, death is the most real thing we know.

What is wrong with not facing death? That approach makes the world a fantasy existence where people never die. The Bible tells us that there is, "...a time to be born and a time to die" (Ecclesiastes 3:2).

The Bible makes many other statements about death that discourage us from taking death lightly. The Bible teaches a certainty to death without ever making it final. Hebrews 9:27 says, "Just as man is destined to die once, and after that to face judgment" (NIV). In the Bible, death doesn't get the last word, however it may seem to us on this side of eternity.
John 11:25 records words Jesus said to a woman who had just buried her brother, "He who believes in me, will live, even though he dies."
So, why do we avoid facing death? Because death scares us!

Freud observed and taught that all of our fears are rooted in the fear of death. We have many fears but in one way or another they can be traced back to our fear of death. When we face our fear of death and overcome that fear, we can face life more completely and realistically.

Imagine living life without fear, or the very least, having less fear.

Perhaps we should make it our personal quest to understand and practice life, liberty, and the pursuit of fearlessness,

Here are some of the fears we face in life:

FEARS

Acrophobia: fear of heights

Xenophobia: fear of foreigners

Ophiciophobia: fear of snakes

Apiphobia: fear of bees

Scotophobia: fear of darkness

Haptpphobia: fear of touching

Stygiophobia: fear of hell

Gymnophobia: fear of nudity

For some, these fears may seem humorous. Others find them very debilitating. Their fears play havoc with their emotions, and they feel like they're on roller coasters, undulating at various speeds while screaming, "No! No!" As the picture suggests, such fears tend to fluctuate wildly and unpredictably. Learning to overcome acrophobia when rock climbing leaves you with a deeper sense of confidence in your abilities and limitations. The process also trains you to trust those who are belaying the ropes. Most rock climbers have a fear of heights. They climb to face their fears.

When we can look at our fears and overcome them, we are free.

We don't deny the fears exist; we decide there are greater reasons to go on with life. Life out of the grip of fear is free. This is what God wants for each of us. It is God's desire that we live lives free in Christ, free from the fear of death, for the fear of death is a slave that affects our lives spiritually, physically, emotionally, and socially. God wants us to live a "life that is truly life" (1 Tim 6:19 NIV). The fear of death is a test of our faith and trust in the hope of the resurrection (this will be covered more fully later).

God's Comfort

As we face death, we can be confident that God will not just leave us alone and in pain. Some will continue seeking to avoid facing death due to the pain. But God is the source of all comfort. As we draw close to Him, we will find peace and joy in our loss and pain. Paul writes the following message to the Corinthians, in his second letter to them:

"All praise to God, the Father of our Lord Jesus Christ. God is our merciful Father and the source of all comfort. He comforts us in all our troubles so that we can comfort others. When they are troubled, we will be able to give them the same comfort God has given us. For the more we suffer for Christ, the more God will shower us with his comfort through Christ. Even when we are weighed down with troubles, it is for your comfort and salvation! For when we ourselves are comforted, we will certainly comfort you. Then you can patiently endure the same things we suffer. We are confident that as you share in our sufferings, you will also share in the comfort God gives us" 2 Corinthians 1: 3-7 (NLT).

Personal Growth and Discussion Questions:

1. Talk to God about your fears and seek His comfort. How has God been a comfort to you in your loss?

2. What other issues have come up between you and God as a result of your loss and pain?

3. Read Psalm 27 and consider how David handled his fears. You may be saying, "This cannot be happening to me," or have fears concerning the future. How does your approach compare with David's?

4. Go off by yourself and write a paragraph or poem about the feelings and fears that you face.

5. Talk to a family member or friend who will listen to what you need to share about your fears. Also share with them things that you've written about your fears. If the person's attitude is, "get over it," then find another person to talk to.

6. Read Matthew 6:25-35. What is the opposite of fear? How are fear and worry related?

7. What do you think you will you need to do or experience in order to cope with your fear and worry?

5

Denial – Wishing it Wasn't So

Denial is our common and sometimes instinctive way of responding to many of the difficult issues we face in life. Not until denial is removed by accepting the issue as real can we deal with the problem as it affects the interior and exterior of our lives. This is true in facing addictions, relational problems, medical issues, and spiritual issues. This is also the case when it comes to death. Acceptance of its reality forces us to engage the issue or problem. Denial or truth each creates a lifestyle. One is a river that flows somewhere, while the other is a dry riverbed of emptiness in life going nowhere.

"No, this can't be true," are often the first words spoken or thought when we receive the "bad news" of a loss. Denial also offers its ostrich-like technique at other times. Denial is the way we try to protect ourselves from the consequences of loss or other issues. Denial is our first line of defense. However, our first task in honestly dealing with death and loss is to accept the reality of the loss.

The human mind will seek to drift into denial whenever it is forced to focus on something that is painful. When we focus on the pain of loss we will continue to be offered the denial method for coping. We may play the mental game called "If only." If only—they had stayed home. If only—they had not been there five minutes longer. If only—etc…this would not have happened. Some may dream of, or imagine a future time when their loved one, who has died, returns. We may imagine that they are on a trip and will return soon, or in six months, or "whatever." In pop culture it's Tupac Shakur's resurrection, or that Elvis may be alive and "in the building" somewhere. Many live in a fantasy world. They choose to live in denial of the obvious.

The movie Corrina, Corrina shows a father who is not coping well with the loss of his wife. He keeps himself busy with work. He cannot face the death and tells his daughter, "Mommy is in the bathtub." Molly, the young daughter, struggles with the loss of her Mommy. Corrina (the housekeeper) spends hours with the daughter, even though she will not talk. One morning as Corrina is making the bed for Molly's Dad, Molly points to her Mom's side of the bed and says, "Corrina, this is where my Mommy sleeps." Corrina hesitates and simply says, "Yes, this is where your Mommy slept". Corrina has to tell her that her Mommy is not coming back. Corrina blows denial away with the truth and allows Molly to begin to deal with a list of emotional issues.

A young friend I'll call April said, almost two years after her mother's death, "I still have not accepted that she is gone. I still expect to eventually come home and see her." April has a group of friends, of which her father does not approve. Her father drinks and is not there emotionally for her, or her sister. She has experimented with drugs, and anger is deeply rooted in her life. April is in denial. Her denial is a desperate attempt to avoid the reality of the loss and opens the way for all kinds of destructive behaviors. For her, to face and accept the loss seems far too painful.

Denial

A viewing or funeral is a designed opportunity to confront denial. For many, seeing the person they love lying in a casket can arrest denial in its tracks. To some, an open casket viewing is painful, but that vivid picture is an open assault on denial. Those who miss a funeral may struggle in this area, for they have no concrete images to check imagination as it wanders into denial. For other losses we need to confront the reality of the loss. If we have lost everything face that reality. We in essence can have a **wake** for the loss of a house, job, or whatever has been lost. We need to acknowledge the loss in front of those we can trust as part of the process of facing the loss.

So, if you lose your job talk to your friends and family about what happened in your life? Withdrawing will not help you or those that you care about. Face it together and commit to making it through the loss. You will need each other like never before.

A young man I know had a dream of being a police officer. He worked hard to attend and pass the police academy. He finished the work and began celebrating and got a DUI. Accepting the reality of the loss for him is to accept that the dream he had has been suddenly killed by the momentary lack of judgment. Denial is a natural reaction in any loss. To face the truth of the loss of a job, loss of the home, the loss of whatever is the first step.

A viewing or funeral is a designed opportunity to confront denial. For many, seeing the person they love lying in a casket can arrest denial in its tracks. To some, an open casket viewing is painful beyond belief. The mental picture in the brain is an threat to future denial. Those who miss funerals and or wakes may struggle in this area. We need concrete proof that the loss is real.

Ways Denial Shows Up

Here are just a few of them:

1.   Not attending funerals and other events that are designed to confront a person with the reality of loss.

2.   Keeping so busy that there is no time to slow down and think. People often hide themselves in an activity or sport.

3.   Refusing to speak about the loss or departed loved one.

4.   Using drugs, alcohol, sex, or other means to escape the pain of the reality.

5.   Playing a head game. For example, pretending that the deceased person has really not died, but is on a trip. Or the

loss is not real and that everything will be fine without facing the facts.

Denial of a loss can lead to further problems; addiction, isolation, deep depression, problems at school and home in relating to people, anger, and rage.

Here are basic tactics to help avoid these pits in the jungle of life:

Ways To Take Down Denial

1.   Confront the loss head-on. Remind yourself that something doesn't have to feel real to be real.

2.   Seek out people to talk to about the loss.

3.   Share the memories of your loved one with those who care about you.

4.   Get together with others on your departed friend's birthday to view videos and pictures of them.

5.   Find people that you can share your struggles with, ones who can understand your experience. This is why a friend or a grief group is vital. (Not the sort that will tell you, "just get over it, man!"

In The Death of Ivan Ilyich, Leo Tolstoy explored his own thoughts on death through writing about the last days of Ivan Ilyich, a man who became ill and wasted away. Through Ivan Ilyich's eyes, the views of a dying man, we experience what it is like to die when those closest to you deny death, especially yours. Tolstoy focuses upon the lie that is told when people are dying. Tolstoy writes,

"Ivan Ilyich suffered most of all from the lie, the lie which, for some reason, everyone accepted: that he was not dying but was simply ill, and that if he stayed calm and underwent treatment he could expect good results. Yet he knew that regardless of what was done, all he could expect was more agonizing suffering and death. And he was tortured by this lie, tortured by the fact that they refused to acknowledge what he and everyone else knew, that they wanted to lie about his horrible condition and force him to become party to that lie. This lie, a lie perpetrated on the eve of his death, a lie that was bound to degrade the awesome, solemn act of his dying to the level of their social calls, their draperies, and the sturgeon they ate for dinner, was an excruciating torture for Ivan Ilyich. And oddly enough, many times when they were going through their acts with him he came within a hairbreadth of shouting: "Stop your lying!" But he never had the courage to do it. He saw that the awesome, terrifying act of his dying had been degraded by those about him to the level of a chance unpleasantness, a bit of unseemly behavior (they reacted to him as they would to a man who emitted a foul odor on entering a drawing room); that it had been degraded by that very "propriety" to which he had devoted his entire life. He saw that no one pitied him because no one even cared to understand his situation."

(Tolstoy, Lev Nicholaevich.. The Death of Ivan Ilvich. New York: 1981, Bantam Books, pp. 102-103).

The lie that Ivan Ilyich's friends and family perpetrated was a result of the denial of death. The people around Ivan Ilyich did not want to admit that his life was ebbing away. Instead they believed, "that he was not dying but was simply ill." Ivan wanted them to care for him, but their lie of denial isolated him from them when he wanted human touch and concern more than anything. Denial of death affects not only the individual denying death, but it prevents us from helping others or being there for others. To fully live we must confront death squarely. Living in denial does not simply inflict pain on ourselves but can often cause pain for those we love. Ironically, Tolstoy himself died alone in a railroad station on a cot (Tolstoy 1981, i). He had always feared dying alone. His fear seems to have come to fruition.

Throughout our global society, we plan for so many issues and future events in life. We plan everything but that which we dread and seek to avoid. A local funeral director told me that less than 10% of people plan for the details of death. Taking care of the details of death is called "pre-arrangement" in the industry. We plan our own and our children's education from cradle to college, and some even plan their spouses and careers. People plan their financial portfolios with just the right ratio of stocks, bonds, and cash, but few plan for that which will come to all of us—the death of ourselves and the death of many we know. Even fewer than the 10% who prearrange funerals, prepare mentally or spiritually for death—their own and that of their loved ones. Only in purchasing burial plots or life insurance are some forced to confront the reality of death. Saving money is one reason that some people give the time of day to such ideas.

We need to be prepared for what is ahead for all of us—death. The most important element is to face death squarely before it shows up at our door. If we are on a airplane that is falling from the sky or in a car soaring over a cliff, it will be to late to face it and come to grips with it. Or even more important, after visiting the doctor and being told you need further tests, and then having the tests show you have a few months left to live. Now is the time to consider how and what you believe about what is beyond death. You can't start treating life seriously until you treat death seriously.

Personal Growth and Discussion Questions:

1. When or how do you think you might fall into thoughts of denial?

2. What effect has your denial had on your life in the past?

3. Why do you let the denial continue? (How are you benefiting from it?)

4. Are you seeing others socially? Do you feel connected with them, or are you in your own little world much of the day?

5. In what ways is your life progressing? Or is it on hold as you deal with the death and loss in your life?

6
What You Should Expect Ahead...

Different people experience life events in different ways. After all, we are all different people—one-of-a-kind in our wiring. Although this is a simple observation, it is not always obvious to everyone. At any rate, grief will affect you in unique, unpredictable ways. In this chapter, I have listed some of the possible ways that I, and others have observed. Do not expect to experience all of the following, but a personal and painful combination of some of these you will surely feel in your grief. They are all components of what is called "normal grief." That means if any of these occur in your life in the next several days, months, and years following your loss, you are normal. Many are surprised by some of the following in their life and they feel strange or weird. Grief has real effects on the emotions, body, and mind. It can produce certain behaviors.

Emotions

Following are some of the emotions that often come with grief:

Sadness—which shows itself in crying. This is an often-feared aspect of grief. Few people want to "loose it" in front of others. But not allowing sadness can cause a more difficult reaction to loss. Allow yourself to feel sadness.

Shock—when you know a person is going to die, shock is less likely. Shock comes when death is sudden and unexpected. From out of nowhere, death appears at the door. Some times when death is expected, when the phone finally call comes, the official word is still a shock.

Numbness—usually sets in after hearing of the death. Some people are unable to feel anything for a while. Their emotions are freeze-dried. This is usually not long-lived.

Anger—is usually experienced some time after the death or loss. Anger, if not owned and dealt with, can lead to difficult problems. Anger can be felt towards the deceased, oneself, or others. The anger turned toward self can lead to depression and suicidal thoughts. Do not blame yourself. Deal with anger in healthy ways.

Guilt—This emotion is usually connected with unkind words, feelings, and or actions close to the time that the person died. These memories, inflated by grief can instigate false guilt. The possibility of real guilt exists if the person was actually responsible for causing the death.

Anxiety—This can range from minor discomfort to major panic attacks. This either comes from fear of not being able to live without the person, or fear of his or her own death.

Fatigue—Grief may leave you feeling drained, exhausted or listless so that you will feel overwhelmed. You will hear others say, "She just sat here all day." Being tired is common, but it can be a sign of clinical depression if it persists.

Helplessness—Death and loss will leave you feeling helpless. There is nothing you can do about the death. You are powerless against this merciless foe. This is a common realization at the onset of grief. That helpless feeling can easily develop into thinking that you will not be able to continue on your own after the loss.

Loneliness—The closer the person was to you, the more likely it is that you will deal with feeling alone. If your loved one was a frequent companion, part of you is gone. Time and space occupied by that relationship is now empty. The result is an alone feeling. Loneliness can be a need for touch from others, or touching others. Even if you wanted to be closer to a friend and now they are gone you can feel lonliness.

Desiring—Wanting to be with the person is a common sign of grief. Cherishing places, objects, music, and movies that remind you of the person, and wanting their company is normal. These desires can develop to being unhealthy. They may cause a person to contemplate their own death as a possible way of joining the one they love.

Free—If the person who died had an emotional or physical hold on or control over you or others, you may experience a sense of release. If the nature of the illness or accident demanded a lot of time and care prior to death, feeling free is a common feeling.

Relief—Feeling at peace because the person dying is no longer suffering. If the relationship with the deceased was painful or difficult, relief is also a common feeling.

Not everyone will feel all of these emotions. These emotions, if they come at all, are not something that we choose. They are listed to let you know if you feel any of these emotions, you are not abnormal. When we think we alone are feeling something, it can alarm or panic some. Every grief is different.

We have to live with the grief as it comes to us and grow through it.

Physical Symptoms

As with the emotions, there is no set pattern for how our bodies will react. The following are some of the physical symptoms and sensations that can come with grief:

1. Dryness of the mouth
2. Hollowness in the stomach or a sense of emptiness
3. Tightness in the throat

4. Tightness in the chest
5. Feeling like you and the world around you are not real but a bad dream
6. Can't get enough air
7. Weakness in the muscles or a lack of strength
8. No tolerance for noise (one person's noise is another person's music)
9. Loss of appetite

This is not a list to check off so much as to understand possible effects. Every loss is different. Talk to your friends and family members about what they are dealing with physically in the months and years after a loss.

Because you are an integrated being, your immune system can become weakened during grief. You may become more susceptible to illness than before. Recognize that your feelings may not simply be grief—you may be sick. Don't hesitate to get help.

Thought Patterns

Following are some of the thought patterns that can come with grief:

Disbelief—This mental pattern, which can occur when a person faces a sudden death. A mother hears that her son, just left home to visit a friend, died in a car crash blocks from the house. Her initial response is an adamant refusal to believe the news. There must be a mistake I just saw him.

Preoccupation—This state of mind characterizes a person who cannot go through a day without replaying, in their minds, conversations, images, and times they had with the person that died. These are not fleeting memories but focused exodus or escape from the rest of living. This becomes critical at work or in school where attention needs to be on the work at hand. You may find yourself listening for a moment but your mind is all of a sudden in another world.

Confusion—Due to disbelief and preoccupation, grieving people may seem "out of it," dazed, or confused. They may say things that seem to make no sense. Certain thoughts may be repeated like a broken record, the same questions asked over and over even whey they have been answered. Often the grieving do not know where they left things, or even how or why they got to a place. This is related to being preoccupied.

Feeling of Presence—Due to their yearning to be with the deceased, those in grief may report strong feelings or convictions that the person or their spirit is with them. Many people feel "watched" by their dead family member or friend for years. They actually believe the person is still immediately with them. The next step is that they feel the person's presence.

Loss affects our thinking to some degree. You are not going crazy if you experience any or all of these thought patterns. People may laugh at you or make jokes but know it is a normal phase. In a culture that fosters "if you believe it, it's true" thinking, these normal by-products of grief can be come the basis for unhealthy long term dysfunction or, as in the case of preoccupation above, create danger for the person or others.

Behaviors

Once again not all of the following may affect you. Look over the list and see how they have affected you and others. It may help you explain some of your own actions and problems or those of your friends and family. Some of the behaviors that often accompany grief:

Eating changes – grief affects many people by altering their appetite patterns. Some eat little or nothing, while others eat more than ever. Sometimes grief can result in major changes in weight.

Sleeping issues - grief can make it either hard to go to sleep, or cause one to wake up early, or in the middle of the night. Sleeping issues are a very common side effect to loss. For some, nightmares can be about death or the person who has died or even dreaming they are with you again.

Absentminded Actions – Your family or friends may scratch their heads at what you do or say. Also they may say to you "hello is anyone there?" This is because grieving people do things that seem out of character. Their preoccupied mental state may make them appear absentminded. They may forget things, lock themselves out of the house or car, miss turns, and forget to turn things on or off. This can be dangerous to themselves and others. This is not a permanent new state; it will correct itself in time and is normal. Be patient with yourself and others.

Withdrawal from others – at some point in the grief process it is very normal for even an outgoing person to appear withdrawn, reserved, quiet, and even solitary when they were the life of the party. People in grief feel ashamed that their emotions and mindset are not normal for them. They may be afraid to loose control in a public place. They may not want to be near people due to their emotions. This will pass with time.

Dreams of the lost loved one – longing, guilt, fear and other emotions are found in your dreams about the deceased. They can be dreams or nightmares, and can last for years.

You are not losing it. This is normal. A young man I will call Carlos lost his cousin due to a drive by shooting in a suburban neighborhood. Neither Carlos nor his cousin, were in a gang. His family blamed him falsely. He struggled with nightmares reliving his cousin's death for several years. Another guy named Robert, who was raised by his grandfather, upon his grandfather's death had vivid dreams that his grandfather would return from a vacation but he would wake up to a grandfather-less world.

Sighing – is a deep gasping for air and then exhaling the air. This is a way to cope with anxiety. Some say that sighing is due to needing more oxygen. Sighing can be an emotional breath of fresh air or a "time out." People in grief often unconsciously use this coping technique for stress relief.

This is vital information for anyone who has friends or family. Teachers are trained in some school districts to notice these signs. Being aware of these clues can help you and those you love. Checkout your friends, are they experiencing some or all of these signs. Remember, you will probably not experience all of these behaviors, feelings, thought patterns, and sensations. But it is important to know, that if you did, it would not be abnormal.

In everyday life, the emotions (of humans) seem to operate under certain laws similar to gravity. As C.S. Lewis describes them in his book, *The Screwtape Letters* (letters 7&8), emotions will follow "the law of undulation." They will follow a pattern of ups and downs, intensity and moderation. In grief, the ups and downs develop a pattern unlike normal life. There will be deep lows and dizzying highs along the way. Remember, you will need others and your Maker on this journey.

Personal Growth and Discussion Questions:

1. Make a list of things from each of these categories you have experienced in dealing with the death of your loved one (When done, go back over the lists). This will need to be done more than once, for as you walk the path of grief, the feelings and all else will change over time.

Feelings_____

Physical Sensations_____

_____

Thought Patterns_____

_____

Behaviors_____

_____

2. Which of these feelings are hardest for you to handle and why?

3. How are your thought patterns affecting your everyday life?

4. Which behavior has bothered you the most? Make a point to share this information with significant people in your life.

7

The Need to Talk About Death

Talking about a loss or a death, as with all communication, is much easier when you feel another person is open to a meaningful conversation. Meaning they are sincerely interested in your thoughts, views, and questions. It is very important, in talking about such difficult subjects as death, to make sure you find a person, or persons, who will listen attentively, respect your views, and answer questions honestly.

Some people find it difficult to verbalize their feelings when someone they love dies. They do a lot of thinking, keeping their questions and conclusions to themselves. They find it hard to begin talking about death, or to even use the word. Why? Because if they do, they will have to admit that the person will no longer be a part of their life.

Most people are intelligent enough to understand that loss and death is inevitable and death is irreversible. Their thinking skills have progressed from the point of seeing cartoon characters fall off of cliffs, after which they get up and walk away, to seeing their pets die, to seeing TV and movies where people die. That does not necessarily mean they want to verbalize their thoughts. This is much harder for some.

In fact, the reason a person does not want to talk about death may be because he or she is working through some of the following issues:

★ Questioning the meaning of life if it is going to end in death. Suddenly, not only death, but the possibility of "beyond death" occupies the mind. Is death a period at the end of a life sentence this is not part of a longer story? If death is a dead end, what really governs life?

★ Getting older as leading inevitably to death. Each day is not a new gift of life but another step closer to the doorway at the end of the hall of life.

★ Seeing death as an enemy. Death becomes personified and hated. The young person may be somewhat surprised that this visceral response is echoed in the Bible.

★ Thinking of them selves as being invincible—"It can't happen to me!" Recklessness often develops from a fatalistic (when your number's up) view of death.

★ Feeling angry at the person for something the person did to them, or they did to the person in the past (i.e. the father deserted the family, had a fight with the person). Now that problem can never be resolved, that offense can never be settled.

★ Feeling guilty because they could have somehow prevented the death or loss.

★ Realizing that they have never developed the necessary coping skills and are unsure how to handle their emotions in public.

Sometimes it takes awhile to find out what is going on deep within another person. They may not even be aware. It may take several questions to get to the root issue. You have to ask questions to understand what another person is going through. Be patient with yourself and others. Care enough to ask good questions. Twice as much listening is required to ask a good question.

When talking to others about death let them talk when they are ready to talk. Do not think of it in terms of a conversation but an ongoing dialogue that takes place over an extended period of time. People need to have people they can open up to over the entire grief period. Not that grief comes to a halt after one to two years but that is a general estimate of what you should expect. If after a few good conversations you do not hear from them—call or reach out to them. They can always tell you they have nothing to say. Most of the time they will say they are glad you took the time to call. stop by, or email.

The friend needs to encourage the person who has had a loss to talk about death or their other losses. Remember, we are all unique individuals. Everything we do and all of our experiences are never the same as anyone else's experiences. What one person needs to talk about is not necessarily what someone else needs to discuss. And family members need to keep in mind that they will not share the same feelings and perceptions, based on their past experiences or current beliefs. When a family member dies, it affects everyone but in a different way. We know that children and adults grieve over divorce in a different way from death. Divorce is a loss that many times keeps on giving grief. This can be due to parental conflicts developed through shared or disputed custody.

I have learned from experience some of the things people need to talk about concerning death. The following questions, asked gently, may release a pent-up reservoir of thoughts and feelings:

⋆ What kind of relationship did you have with the person who died? –Sometimes a person will feel that the person who died was the only one who really understood them, or possibly supported them in times of trouble. They need to talk about their feelings of aloneness or fears of not having the person in their life.

⋆ As you think about your loved one, how would you describe the "unfinished business" part of your relationship? What issues do you wish had been resolved?

★ Sometimes people feel as if the person who died got away with something. They escaped some consequences for things they did. How do you relate to that possibility? Perhaps they feel guilty of how they feel, because the person may have been abusive to them or their mother.

Special Circumstances:

★ When a loss or death is sudden, violent, and unexpected it involves traumatic feelings. These situations most assuredly require immediate attention and intervention. They may even require professional counseling. Schools often provide grief counselors after tragedies that affect a student community. These are often voluntary, and a more direct approach may be required from those who notice the effects in a grieving person's life.

★ When you are directly involved with a death, this experience is also traumatic. You may have been a witness to a violent accident or a preventable death like drowning. Something you knew, should have said, or done ahead of time may leave you feeling somewhat responsible. These can be difficult feelings to share with someone else, particularly if you think they may hold you responsible.

★ The dying person may have wanted you to do something after they died. Someone, usually a parent or relative, may have said something to the effect, "Now I don't want you to go around feeling bad after I'm gone." Or "Don't cry over me." They may have even left instructions that the family was not to have a funeral. These people do not understand that they are not allowing the people left behind, and who love them, to do what needs to be done. They are trying to withhold the necessary opportunity to grieve, talk about them, and say a final good-bye. These same people might as well ask the sun not to rise.

★ A person definitely needs to talk about "How is the death of the person going to affect my future?" Life style and immediate plans are things that can drastically change with the death of a parent, especially the parent who brings home the support. Career possibilities (i.e. college) planned for by the student can suddenly be interrupted or altered.

As you are able to talk about death, and how it is affecting you, you will be developing the self-awareness you need to get yourself through a very difficult time. Make sure you make your needs apparent and clear by verbalizing them. Ask for any type of help that will get you through this troubling time. Respect your limitations and be willing to allow others into your life who are willing to listen when you have the need to talk about death.

Personal Growth and Discussion Questions:

1. How difficult is it for you to talk about death? Why?

2. In what circumstances have people, especially relatives, discussed the subject of death with you before? How have those discussions helped or hindered you?

3. What issues do you think might keep you from wanting to talk about death?

4. Do you feel that there was anything unique or different about how the person died, compared to other deaths you've known about?

5. How has the person's death altered or changed your life in any way?

8
Your Responsibility in Grief

Love does not die. Wealth can be lost. Homes passed on to others. People and pets do. The grief process begins with a terrible and lonely loss. Grief may change you but it won't destroy you. Grief can be a very powerful teacher. In the process of assuming responsibility for your grief, I want to encourage you to take small baby steps and take joy in even the smallest victories.

Grief is a process. Getting better is your choice. A friend once told me that, "Grief is the price you pay for having loved someone deeply." He was right, but you do not have to go on paying that price forever. Love itself can gradually return to center stage. You will endure this worst of all kinds of experiences. I have worked through several of them and can promise you that you, too, will survive. There is hope.

As I've listened to survivors tell their stories, many of which involve the details of how their loved ones died, I've realized that no story has been the same; neither has their grief.

If, at the moment, you do not feel brave or strong, do not force it. Dealing with your grief means assuming responsibility for it. And assuming responsibility requires that you take care of yourself in some important ways. Here are some that might help:

★ Accept the fact that grief is normal. Know that you can, and will, heal from your grief. Grief will affect all of you in some way. It does not just affect your emotions.

★ Involve yourself in times of remembering, commemorating the loss of your loved one (i.e. memorial services, funerals, and any traditions of your culture). If possible, contribute a thought, memory, or tribute. Honor the life of the person who died.

★ Be with others, especially during the first hours, days and weeks of your grief. Family and friends are there for support. Do not isolate yourself from them. At some point you will feel that no one understands. Others will not understand unless you tell the people you trust.

★ Talk about the person and their death when you can. No one should feel pressured to talk, but it is helpful to tell your story and share your personal feelings about what has happened.

★ Express yourself somehow. Even if you don't feel like talking, find ways to express your thoughts and emotions (i.e. a journal, song, poem, or eulogy about the person who died). You can do this just for yourself, or to share with others. Writing your thoughts out first and asking someone to read them for you can be the start of expression. You can even write a letter to the deceased to get your feelings out.

✴ Exercise and eat right—even when you don't feel like it. Grief is exhausting and it is important to stay healthy. Be careful not to use alcohol, drugs, or tranquilizers. These will only mask the pain and could lead to other problems. Exercise has a lot to do with our moods, and your body needs nutritious foods to keep it healthy, especially through stressful times. You may feel like just eating junk food or skipping meals, but this is a very important part of assuming responsibility for yourself during your grieving.

✴ It is important to take time for rest. Try to develop regular times to go to bed. It is a fact that the hours prior to midnight count twice as much as the hours after midnight. If you are having trouble getting to sleep, try listening to easy, soothing music. Meditation and prayer can also help you to get the rest you need.

✴ Establish and/or maintain a routine. People do not operate at peak levels during their grieving period, but try, as best you can to do your regular chores. Some chores can wait, while others may impact the routine of other family members.

✴ Do not suppress your emotions. Work through, express, or release them. Have a "good cry" if you feel one coming on. Go to a private place and scream or punch a punching bag.

✴ Attend church services and stay in touch with your "extended family," particularly if they have been a continuing source of support for you. Realize, however, that even pastors lack "extrasensory" perception—they may only know what you tell them.

★ Find other good books or articles on the grieving process, so they can help you identify what you are feeling and give you ideas on how to assume responsibility for your grief.

★ And finally, join a support group. Ask a counselor or pastor to recommend one, and get involved. The thing to remember is, don't be alone with your feelings and pain. It is very difficult to grieve alone.

The main reason for being with others during the grieving process is because part of growing through grieving is telling the story of the loss. If you don't have other people to tell the story to, you may find it difficult to move along your journey through grief.

We would hope that our journey would be over in a matter of weeks or months. Unless you have experienced loss before, you may be unaware of how to assume the responsibility of working through it. If this is your first time, it may be intense, and you may feel that you will never get through it. However, there will come a time when you will be able to get through a day without crying or thinking of the person or pet with a deep longing to see, hold, or talk to them. But you will never forget them or the experience of having to assume the responsibility for your grief.

Personal Growth and Discussion Questions:

1. What are some of the changes you've had to make in order to adjust to the loss of your loved one?

2. What do you think it means that, "Grief is the price you pay for having loved someone deeply?"

3. What is one way you have found it difficult in assuming responsibility for your grief?

4. Where do you feel you need help in assuming responsibility for your grief?

5. What have you read or listened to since the death of your loved one? Do you have a journal, or have you written a poem, song, or eulogy you would like to share with others because it helped you in some way?

6. What other ways you have discovered that have helped you to assume responsibility for your grief?

9

As If the Loss Was Not Bad Enough –Secondary Losses

Jan a high school student, who was recommended by a teacher to attend the grief group, which I coached at her local high school. She had just lost her mother due to cancer. She moved to my town to live with her father and her stepmother. The difficult move was necessary, because she had no one in the city where they had lived following her mother's death. The move created even more loss in her life because she had to leave all her friends behind. Just as she started to adjust to a new school and make new friends, her father got sick and also died. Jan had to move again to a second new city to live with another relative. She was living a nightmare caught in a chain of losses. There was the primary loss followed by many secondary losses. Within a short time she had become an orphan. Along the way she had experienced repeated painful losses.

For Jan, these secondary losses were real and devastating. It was bad enough to lose Mom, but she lost so much more. Even before

Mom's death, preliminary losses had started piling up. Jan lost her home due to her mother not being able to afford the house payments.

Then she lost all her friends when they moved to a more affordable town. She got into a fight with her best friend and that relationship was over. The loss of her best friend hurt the most out of the secondary losses. The losses that followed almost defeated her. In almost any major loss there are other smaller losses that follow.

The primary loss is often times like a sucker punch. It comes out of nowhere. It feels like a knock out blow. The secondary losses have a pummeling effect on a person's life (like repeated punches to the face and body). Primary losses send us to the mat for a mandatory count. Will we get up again? If we do, are we ready for the fight that will resume?

Oftentimes we can brace for a loss if a parent or friend is seriously ill. Few anticipate the secondary losses. Some of these losses are logical and predictable, while others are completely unexpected.

The proverbial straw that breaks the camel's back is a fitting illustration for the effects of pummeling from secondary loss. Is it any wonder that a person feels beat-up during a time of grief?

Another scenario involves the guy who loses his father through cancer. He is deeply in pain and needs a person to care about his feelings. Instead of support, Mom is also in deep grief from losing her husband. To that High School student who lost Dad it also feels like he lost Mom too. Mom may be physically alive but at the moment dead in her ability to emotionally support her son. Mom spends time alone in her room and comes home late. At times she drinks and yells in pain.

Then in time, if mom dates and the new boyfriend does not appreciate the son, the son feels like a foreigner in his own home. When and if the new boyfriend becomes a step-dad, accepting this change involves further grief. Many times there is conflict between son and the new guy who tries to act like his dad. This only makes the loss of his real father all the more painful.

Grief from primary and secondary losses is real and different for each of us. The first loss is bad; the second, third, fourth, and on can nearly wipe us out emotionally. The danger is that the first loss will not be grieved thoroughly, but the grief will be arrested—left unfinished to be dealt with later. This has been called delayed grief. This can cause problems years later. Grief has caused anxiety attacks years later. A grief that has not been worked through will often times be too painful to talk about or face even decades later.

Personal Growth and Discussion Questions:

1. What secondary losses have you experienced?

2. Which secondary loss affected your life the most?

3. How were you prepared or unprepared for the secondary losses?

4. How are coping now?

5. If this happened to you—when one loss is followed by others…How did the first loss get buried in the other losses you experienced?

6. If this is hard for you to see, go back to the losses in your life in the exercises at the end of chapter one. Do you see patterns in your own loss history?

10

How Do I Understand Grief?

What is grief? It is the reaction of a whole person to loss. Grief affects the whole person. Grief is experienced, to varying degrees, in all losses. Since people are made up of physical, social, emotional, mental, and spiritual components, each of these areas is affected in grief. For the most part, we associate grief with emotions, but it touches the whole of a person. These elements (physical, emotion, social, and spiritual) of a person are like notes, and each person's grief composes a different song, which is "played" throughout our lives. Hence, we cannot expect any two people to respond alike or even in a similar way. Even the same individual experiences different losses (deaths, etc.) with different grief reactions and intensities. William Worden who developed the four tasks of grief wrote,

"Physically, death has an effect on people. It is common for grieving people to feel sick, weak, or have a feeling of hollowness in the gut. Some experience dryness of mouth and tightness in the throat or chest. There is crying, loss, or increase of appetite, weakness, and lack of energy. Sleep patterns may also be altered, while others experience nightmares. The physical effects can last days, weeks, months, and even years. The physical effects can be unique, as is everyone." (Worden 2001, 15-18)

Grief usually begins in our emotions, with shock and sadness as the most frequent and immediate feelings. Nevertheless, deep emotions often follow for days, months, or years. Some of the other emotions include: loneliness, anger, anxiety, guilt, listlessness, helplessness, relief, freedom, dumbness, and depression. To feel these emotions can be normal and common. Being stuck in one or more of these emotions is also possible, but not healthy. Dealing with our emotions is very important. We can deal with them in healthy ways or create future trials due to the method we choose to deal with these emotions.

There are also significant social implications of death and grief on everyday life. These are different for each person. The main social structures of family, circles of friends, churches and governments are all affected. The structure and cohesion of a family may be shattered or altered by a death. A circle of friends will be forever different with the loss of a member of the circle. Death affects the roles we play in social interactions. Death has social implications for everyone. For some it is a different group of people to live with. We lose friendships due to a move that results from the death of the family provider.

Spiritually, death has a deep spiritual affect on everyone. At some point in a life, it might even contribute to a crisis. Several losses can add up to unexpected personal consequences. An historical example can be seen in the life of C. S. Lewis. He wrote exhaustively about the spiritual affect in his book, A Grief Observed. In 1994, when Anthony Hopkins played C. S. Lewis in the movie, *Shadowlands*, this spiritual affect was made very public. C. S. Lewis had lost his mother at a young age, and his father after years of conflict (Lewis 1955, 18). He also lost a close friend in World War I and another dear friend after World War II, Charles Williams. These deaths were difficult, but nothing like the loss of Joy Davidman Lewis, his wife and love of his life. She was a Christian, and so was Jack (C.S. Lewis' nick name) Lewis. Lewis' faith was tested to its core. His faith, in the end, proved true and able to face the stark reality of this deep loss (Lewis 1961, 1-5). The furnace of loss and suffering tested his faith, as if by fire. The impurities became evident. At every personal loss, our faith is tested. "Is God in control, or is life out of control?" This is a common question in moments of crisis. "Does God care? Did God cause this loss?" Or simply "Why?" These are all common points of spiritual crisis.

Even those who hold other beliefs about death find that a worldview is untested and unsure until faced by the reality of loss. Do the spiritual answers we hold onto stand up to the realities of life, especially death? Grief forces us to examine and re-evaluate the answers to which we cling for life and death's meaning. Spiritually, in the grief process, faith is either deepened or questioned and oftentimes both.

How Should We Respond to Those Who Grieve?

Many churches have sadly taken on the approach of our culture in regards to the area of grief. Instead of starting with Scripture, some have taken hold of Kuebler-Ross alone. Other leaders have allowed their weaknesses to be a norm for a whole congregation. Some theological perspectives, when it comes to grieving, seek to make denial of grief a standard. They say things like, "You know where they are going, Why are you so broken-up over this loss?" They quote a few scriptures (without the rest) that we are not to grieve as the world grieves. They are really saying, "you should not hurt; just get over it." Another common saying is, "Your deep sense of loss shows that you were too attached to that person. God wants to have first place in your heart." There may be spiritual lessons to learn, but timing is everything. Is grieving portrayed in Scripture as a sign of weakness only for weak believers? What is the Biblical view of grief? Let us examine some of the most important passages about grief from the Scriptures.

The Origin of Grief

Grief began in Genesis (the first book of the Bible) as one of the affects of the fall of man. Before death, there was only joy, peace, and security. Grief wasn't necessary. But death brought grief, pain, and toil into human reality. The first experience of death and grief was recorded in Genesis 4 when Cain killed his brother Abel. Adam and Eve felt grief for the first time. It must have been a shock and a horror that was beyond their understanding. Adam and Eve understood death intellectually. God told them that they would, "surely die," but grief had never been for them a reality. They had known the pain and grief of their own remorse and guilt for their sin. This pain of grief from death was new. Their grief must have been gut wrenching. They had never grown up seeing others experience this pain for it was new.

In the Bible, the first time we see the word for grief occurs when God was grieved over the Earth before the flood. Genesis 6:7 records, "So the Lord said, I will wipe mankind, whom I have created, from the face of the earth—

men and animals, and creatures that move along the ground, and birds of the air—for I am grieved that I have made them." God was grieved that he had made man. Noah and his sons grieved over the loss of the world and their sense of safety. Their thinking must have been along these lines, Will we be safe in the future or will this happen again unexpectedly? God blessed and encouraged them to be fruitful and multiply. To give them confidence, he made a covenant with them (Genesis 9:9-17 NIV). Grief is recorded and found throughout the pages of Scripture (for the Bible reflects real life).

It is important to remember that Jesus wept openly for his friend Lazarus. His tears and weeping were so heavy that it moved those at Lazarus' home. Grief is neither for the weak, nor a sign of weakness. Even the Son the Man, the Son of God wept. Tears are not a sign of weakness in humans, but a sign of love and compassion. Jesus also spoke words of comfort to Mary and Martha. He said, "I am the Resurrection and the Life."

Personal Growth and Discussion Questions:

1. Where did grief come from in your understanding?

2. How does grief affect a human beings from your experience?

3. How has grief affected you socially (your family and circle of friends)?

4. How has grief affected you physically?

5. How has grief affected you mentally?

6. How has grief affected you spiritually?

7. Are you happy about your faith or have you become angry or disappointed through your grief experiences?

11

How Do You See Death?

I remember seeing a picture of an embalmed man clutching the steering wheel of his Cadillac as he was lowered, in the car, into his grave. He obviously thought he might drive it again, or he was going to make sure that no one else would be driving the car. Have you noticed that very few hearses travel down the road pulling a U-Haul trailer? The bottom line is that you cannot take stuff with you. To most, this is only a joke. In ancient times, some people thought that this was no joke. How you view death affects how you live life.

Over the centuries, people have viewed death in various ways.
The Egyptians thought that if you prepared for eternity, you could enjoy it. Many in Egypt spent the majority of their lives preparing for the life beyond. Their bodies had to be prepared in a lengthy process of mummification that took skill and great cost. They would pay the price.

They believed they could take things with them into the next world. Archeologists have spent hundreds of years digging up their preparations for the next world. We can study what they wanted to take with them. Pharaohs had their servants killed so they could accompany them in to the future along with their dogs and pets.

So, those Egyptians who believed this spent most of their lives, as if they could prepare for the life beyond. They committed their time and wealth to their belief that, what they prepared would be of use in the next world. Almost no one today believes that you can take it with you. The common views today are the following three answers to the question:

What Happens After a Person Dies?

This is a vitally important question. It can bring a person hope or leave that person in despair. Your understanding of this question will set the course of your mental and spiritual journey. The answer should flow from your worldview or philosophy of life. Coming to grips with life is the first step in facing death (of others and our own). Death is a part of life. An examination of the various religious beliefs and philosophies through the ages will reveal three main views of death. Each of these views will be briefly considered, as well as the results of
living by these world views.

Materialism: Only Worm Food

This view states that this life is all there is. When we die, that's it – it is just plain over. We become dust, or worm food. There is no more life and no hope for further life. In this view, reality is limited to the five senses. This means that there is no hope in death. Death is the Mother of all losses. As with every idea of death this view affects how we live. For example, it leads many to party hardy. The Epicureans of ancient
Greece held this view; thus their motto was, "eat, drink and be merry for tomorrow we shall die." A modern version might be, enjoy fun now, for when death comes the worms alone will party.

Reincarnation: Butterfly or Cow?

Another common view is reincarnation, the belief that a new body and a new life follow after this life. Popularized in movies since the 1960's, this view holds that the way a person lived in a previous life affected this life. The next life is determined by the Karma (good or bad) that a person receives because of the way he or she lives right now. In fact, that person could be a better human or a cow or a monkey in the next life.

This affects how we live in several ways. First of all, we probably will try to live a good life – bring food to the temples, and so forth. Hindus, and some Buddhists, hold this view. They believe that god is in everything. Everything is god. So a mouse or a monkey can be divine.

We are part of god. When we die it is like a drop of water as it is dropped into a glass of water. The drop is lost within the whole glass.

Individuality is of little importance. Death and pain are an illusion.

Mother Teresa came to India where this view of life and death reigned. She found people near death on the streets of Calcutta. She had compassion on them. She carried them in off the street removed the maggots, washed them, fed them, held them, and loved them as they died. This is why Mother Teresa became so famous. She valued the people whom the Hindu society did not value. She challenged a worldview with compassion. The Hindu mind looks at poverty as the result of bad karma from a previous life. This is, in part, why social responsibility has been a foreign concept within some societies. Whatever a person thinks about death affects the way that person lives.

Resurrection: You Get a New Life

Jews, Christians, and Muslims all believe that, after death, eventually a person's body will arise again, not a different body but the same one with new life. In Ezekiel's vision, dry bones in the desert spring back to life (Ezekiel 37:1–14). The well-known spiritual, about "them dry bones" has popularized the vision ("The anklebone 's connected to the foot bone; the foot bone's connected to the leg bone – now hear the Word of the Lord"). Christianity is based on the historical (in time and space), physical resurrection of Jesus of Nazareth – Jesus came back to life after being dead and placed in a tomb for three days. In I Corinthians 15:12–19, Paul the Apostle said that this event forms the foundation of the Christian faith.

How can such varied views be tested to be true or false?

Digging up dead bodies does not prove the materialist view. It only proves that the body decays, and all views hold to this. Talking to people who claim to be tigers or past world leaders in previous lives is not proof of reincarnation. Some believe it only proves mental instability. The only real proof would be for someone who has died to come back to life and speak of the experience.

Personal Growth and Discussion Questions:

1. Talk to your pastor or youth pastor about this issue. Call his or her office and set up an appointment.

2. Read, *The Case for Christ*, by Lee Strobel (Grand Rapids, MI: Zondervan Publishing House; ISBN: 0310226465).

3. Read I Corinthians 15 and discuss this chapter with a Christian friend.

4. What views in this list can you match with people you have known? What view about life and death do you hold? Why?

5. How is your view of death affecting the way you live?

6. If you have not made a decision about you believe about the after life what keeps you confused or unsure?

12

Living Life in View of Death

A number of years ago a man picked up the morning paper and, to his horror, read his own obituary. "Have I died?" he asked himself. The newspaper had reported the death of the wrong man. The caption read: "Dynamite King Dies." The story identified him as a "merchant of death." He was the inventor of dynamite and he had amassed a great fortune from the manufacture of weapons of destruction. Moved by this disturbing experience, he radically changed his commitment to life. A healing power greater than the destructive force of dynamite came over him. He was a changed man. Thereafter, he committed his full energy and money to works of peace and making life better for all humanity. Today he is best remembered as the founder of the Nobel Peace Prize -- Alfred Nobel.

Paul wrote to Timothy to speak in a challenging way to people that had the wrong idea about life and happiness:

Command those who are rich in this present world not to be arrogant nor to put their hope in wealth, which is so uncertain, but to put their hope in God, who richly provides us with everything for our enjoyment. Command them to do good, to be rich in good deeds, and to be generous and willing to share. In this way they will lay up treasure for themselves as a firm foundation for the coming age, so that they may take hold of the life that is truly life. Timothy, guard what has been entrusted to your care. Turn away from godless chatter and the opposing ideas of what is falsely called knowledge, which some have professed and in so doing have wandered from the faith. Grace be with you" (I Timothy 6:17-21 NIV).

What is life that can truly be called life? It is not living for wealth and possessions but living and putting hope in God and the hope of the life to come. Living with this kind of hope allows a person to face death with sorrow and with hope, for the loss is not the end of the story.

In the movie, SecondHand Lions, two unusual uncles take in a displaced boy—their nephew. The uncles have a new start on life due to his introduction into their lives. The past defeats had limited their view of the future and the worth of others in their lives. Most people live only in view of what drives them. For some it is to excel others to survive, and for others it to enjoy life to its fullest. As an old circus lion gets a second chance, so do these old uncles. Many of us are like the old uncles—just living. With the introduction of purpose and hope into their lives, they began living life to the fullest. When they died, it was said that they had really lived.

What is "living in view of death?" Many people refuse to consider that their days are numbered, or that there is a limit to the length of their lives. The cold reality is that life is short. As James writes, life is like a vapor. We are reminded of this at the news of every death in the paper or on the Internet. Yet, we ignore the fact until the death of a person close to us strikes, and the reality clicks in our brains and emotions.

Chuck Swindoll tells a true story that comes from the sinking of the Titanic. It is not a story of love, romance, and more.

A nervous old woman found her place in a lifeboat that was about to be lowered into the icy raging North Atlantic. She suddenly thought of something she needed, so she asked permission to return to her stateroom before they were lowered into the frigid waters. The crew member gave her three minutes before they would have to leave without her. She ran up the deck that was already slanted at a steep angle. She raced through the gaming room with all the money that had slid to one side, ankle deep. She did not stoop to grab any of the coins both gold and silver. She came to her stateroom and quickly pushed aside her diamond rings and expensive bracelets and necklaces as she reached to the shelf above her bed and grabbed three small oranges. She made her way back to the lifeboat and sat down. Before the Titanic hit the iceberg she would not have considered a crate of oranges for even the smallest pinky ring. When death entered the picture her priorities changed. One blast of its awful breath had transformed all values. The priceless things had become worthless. Worthless things had become priceless. And in that moment she preferred three small oranges to a crate of diamonds"

The point is that death has and will enter your life now and again in the future. Life is short. How will you live your life? What do you want to accomplish? What do you want said of you at the end of life's journey? What will your obituary say? After living a full life, what do you want to be said of your life? Only you can determine what you want said. The most you can do is aim at the direction you want your life to take.

The writer Frederick Buechner, wrote this about life:

The temptation is always to reduce it to size: A bowl of cherries. A rat race. Amino acids. Even to call it a mystery smacks of reductionism. It is the mystery.

As far as anybody seems to know, the vast majority of things in the universe do not have whatever life is. Sticks, stones, stars, space—they simply are. A few things are and are somehow aware of it. They have broken through into Something, or Something has broken through into them, even a jellyfish, or a butternut squash. They're in it with us. We're all in it together, or it in us. Life is it. Life is with.

After lecturing learnedly on miracles, a great theologian was asked to give a specific example of one. "There is only one miracle," he answered. "It is life."

Have you wept at anything during the last year?

Has your heart beat faster at the sight of a young beauty?

Have you thought seriously about the fact that some day you are going to die?

More often than not do you really listen when people are speaking to you instead of just waiting for your turn to speak?

Is there anybody you know in whose place, if one of you had to suffer great pain, you would volunteer yourself?

If your answer to all or most of these questions is "no," the chances are that you're dead (Wishful Thinking, page 51).

Diogenes was a renowned pagan thinker living in Greece. One day he set up a tent in the marketplace of Athens with a sign, which read: "Wisdom sold here."

One of the citizens laughed at the idea, and sent a servant with twelve cents in Greek money, saying: "Go and ask that braggart how much wisdom he will let you have for twelve cents." When the servant delivered the money and message to Diogenes, the latter answered: "Tell this to your master: 'In all your actions look to the end.'"

When the servant brought home this message, his master was so pleased with it, that he had the words painted in gold over the entrance of his house so that he and everyone else entering his house might be reminded of the end of life. Even the mere natural virtue seemed to him so valuable. In I Peter 4:4 we read, "Be prudent therefore and watchful in prayers." Arthur Tonne, Lent And The Seven Virtues, (Didde Printing, Emporia, KS, 1956), p. 26.

We need to live our lives in view that we will die. Life is short even if we live to be a 100! This fact alone should affect the way we live our lives.

Personal Growth and Discussion Questions:

1. What will be said about your life by those who gather at your funeral?

2. Do you pass time or really live life?

3. When death enters your life, when death becomes non-fiction, how will your priorities change?

4. What is it that you thought was valuable, but due to the invasion of death in your life, now seems trivial?

5. Do you look to the end of life everyday? What keeps you from thinking about your death and reaching your final goals?

13
Grief, School or Work

When grief strikes, school or work is often the last thing you want to deal with due to the pain. You do not want to be around people because you are not sure that you can hold yourself together. You might just burst into uncontrollable tears. This may be your fear.

If a friend or family member is terminally ill, contact your school counselor or employer, and ask if there are grief groups to help cope with loss. If there is one, and attend the group meetings. If there is not one as yet, consider going to one outside of school or work at a hospital, funeral home, or place of worship – church. This will help you realize that you are not alone in what you are going through.

If sudden death strikes, also contact your school counselor or employer and alert them of your loss. Before going back to school or work full time consider going back for a brief visit. Get your missed assignments and have lunch or go to your favorite class or work part of the day. Then when you are ready to go for the full day, know how to contact your parents, grandparents, and or family friend in case it is emotionally to much for you. On your first full day back talk to each teacher make sure they know why you were absent and ask them for their support as you go through this tough time. You have a real need to have added emotional support. If this is to hard for you to talk about, write a teacher a short note, telling them of your loss. This will help them understand that you just did not feel like going to school. This can be very simple on your computer or send them an email.

Due to the affects of grief on you, mentally, school may be a different kind of challenge in the days, weeks, and months ahead. Where you always remembered the assignments and did them automatically, now you may totally miss assignments. You were in class, you sat at the desk, you remember parts of what the teacher said, but there were moments when you were sitting but gone. Your mind had wondered. You were thinking of the person you lost and times in the past that you spent together.

Expect that during the time you are grieving, it will be harder to concentrate on any subject, to remember information, and to organize what you have learned in order to complete your homework assignments. Do not be shocked if your grades drop. Let your parents know this and your friends and especially let yourself know it, so you don't beat yourself up. Grieving the loss of a loved one makes it harder, much harder to keep your mind focused. All you can think of is your loved one who has died. You may daydream in the middle of a very important and interesting project, or a time with your friends, possibly even at a sporting event. You may be there, but your mind might be a million miles away. In class, in practice or after school, the teacher or coach calls out your name and you are startled. Your class, or the rest of the team laughs and you may feel stupid. Remember there is nothing wrong with you. This, because of your grief, is normal. Be patient. Your teachers may not know about a death or loss in your life. Make sure you let them know. Do not expect them to put you on a sheltered path. They will grade you the same, but they will be more understanding. Expect variations in your academic or athletic performance, when you are grieving. Often, this does not last long. If you experience these kinds of problems, remember that, in time, your grades or performance will pick up again. Allow yourself time to grieve. The daydreaming is part of grieving. You do not need to be in isolation but you need to understand and be prepared to help others understand what is going on inside of you.
The following is a brief checklist of practical and helpful contacts and actions you can take during grief:

• Communicate with your friends, parents, teachers, and coaches.
Let them know how things are for you, and ask for extra time or additional help. Let them know that you are finding it hard to focus.

• You may need to change your study habits. Allow yourself more time to complete your homework. Try changing study habits to fit your energy and attention levels. If before you did it late at night, try getting up early to do some of your studying while you mind is fresh and there are fewer distractions. This may require that you go to bed earlier.

• If all of a sudden you are forgetful, even forgetting very important things, write them down. Trust what you wrote, not your memory. Buy a small notebook for this purpose. Things will not get better but worse if you use scraps of paper, napkins, or receipts, as they tend to get lost. Ask your friends or coaches to call you and remind you of important events.
People who care about you want to help, but you have to let them know what help you need.

• If what you are studying is not getting inside your head, try reading out loud to yourself. (It's best to do this when alone.) You will remember the spoken words as well as the written, and the information will sink in better. I did this during a dark period in my own college days, with great success.

• It may have been that before, you had a chapter down in one reading. Now as a result of grief, read the pages quickly for overall content, and then reread them carefully, underlining or highlighting important passages. Allow yourself extra time. Some students find it hard to concentrate on school. Others lose themselves in the work to avoid the emotional pain. Everyone is a little different. By observing how you handle loss you will be prepared to make little choices in daily living that will keep you going and growing.

Personal Growth and Discussion Questions:

1. How has your experience of grief affected your school work or work after school?
2. Ask people who are in your class and you trust or people you work with what they have noticed. What is it they noticed about you since the loss in your life?
3. Have you told your teachers or school counselor about your loss? If not why not?
4. What is it that causes you to hesitate telling others?
5. Is there anything about school sports practice or work that could be dangerous for you and others if your attention is compromised?
6. Is there one teacher or coach that it would be easier to tell?
7. Does your school have a grief group? Ask your counselor about this. Set up an appointment if necessary. Another approach is to have your youth pastor make contact for you at school.

14
Remembering the Lost

The fourth step of working through grief is putting the person whom you have lost in a new place in your heart and memory. As we noted in Chapter One,

Task IV: Emotionally Assign a New Place in Your Memory and Heart to the Person or Relationship(s) (Value or Self-Concept you had based on a job or material things) & Move on With Life.

Will you Miss me When I'm Gone?

Carter Family

VERSE 1

When death shall close these eyelids

An' th heart shall stist to be

When they lay me down to rest

In some flowery boundry tree

CHORUS:

Will you miss me, will you miss me

Will you miss me, will you miss me when I'm gone

We all want to be remembered when we are gone. Also, we want to remember those we have lost. There are some things that you can never forget. Then there are memories that fade. For a while, looking at a photograph or perhaps a video will restore our memory. Over the years the memories begin to fade. C.S. Lewis, the author of The Lion, the Witch, and the Wardrobe, wrote concerning this after losing his wife to cancer. He recorded his feelings in three notebooks, which later became the book A Grief Observed.

I have no photograph of her that's any good. I cannot even see her face distinctly in my imagination. Yet the odd face of some stranger seen in a crowd this morning may come before me in vivid perfection the moment I close my eyes tonight. No doubt, the explanation is simple enough. We have seen the faces of those we know best so variously, from so many angles, in so many lights, with so many expressions—waking, sleeping, laughing, crying, eating, talking, thinking—that all the impressions crowd into our memory together and cancel out into a mere blur. But her voice is still vivid. The remembered voice-—hat can turn me at any moment to a whimpering child. (C. S. Lewis, *A Grief Observed*, New York: Bantam, 1976, pp.16-17).

We never want to forget the loved one that leaves our lives. We want always to remember the person, the relationship, and the fun times. We long to see the smile or the laugh of the loved that is sorely lost.

In time, the memory fades and it becomes difficult to picture them in our mind. My friend Matt that died in his twenties six months after finding cancer on his tongue is still in my heart and mind. I have not seen him in forty years but there is still a fuzzy image in my thoughts. I know it is not detailed. I know he wouldn't recognize me today and he would look different if he had lived. He left my life back then. Faded memory is all that I have. I remember his joy, his smile, his tears, and his love of life. I hold in my heart the hope of seeing him in heaven. In the meantime, now pictures just are not any good.

Another example is my grandfather Council Best, who died in 1961. He will always be my grandfather. The years do not change that. The same is true with everyone we lose no matter how close or significant. My grandfather now is in my life but in an inactive place. The memories are "on demand" and able to fill my mind at will. New memories are never added. The old is there and I have come to accept that. And the memories that are there fade.

Another way to explain this same reality is… do you remember when you were Middle School you had some friends that you do not have now? Those people even your best friends at the time are still part of your life, but they may not all be an active part of your current life experience. They are like my dead grandfather, even though they may be alive somewhere on the planet or beyond. They are in my life but not an active participant in my life. This is the place we need to move those we lose.

Who is it in your life that once was an important or unimportant part that is missed now due to loss? Can you name several? Not only from death but through life changes—moving, breakups, and other loses. Handle those memories in a deliberate way. Honor those personal influences in your life by the way you remember them.

Some memories are painful in the sense that they make us feel sad, angry, and even guilty. How do we handle feelings like this? Mostly, we have to live through them, remembering that the way we feel isn't necessarily the last word on reality. Our feelings aren't the whole picture. But the picture can be overwhelming. Sometimes memories are living nightmares while other memories fill us with joy, a deep laugh, or wet eyes of happiness. A little of both extremes are the reality that make up our memories of most people.

For some, the tendency in dealing with a loved one's death is to focus on the good and only on the good. The result is that we turn the human being we lived with into a faultless saint. The person is then not remembered (as they were), but as we want to, or think we have to remember them. If we want to be faithful to our friends and loved ones we need to remember them, as we actually knew them. This means looking at a balanced set of memories. The person that we are thinking about who has died had both strengths and weaknesses. We need to remember both extremes and everything in between. This takes effort and the input of others.

There is great benefit in taking time to sit and remember the good and bad experiences as well as the strengths and weaknesses of those we have lost. Other people that knew them can give us another and broader perspective. Listen as carefully as possible to others when they speak about your loved one. Beyond the clichés and required statements you will often catch moments of great good done by someone you knew. This is the importance of stories during times of grief. They are always better than a list of qualities. Instead of hearing that he or she was a really caring person, we would rather hear about a vivid moment when someone felt deeply cared for by our loved one. As we truthfully examine our memories of someone we will admit there are things we miss and things we do not miss about them. They may have been persistently unable to get anywhere on time, but that flaw seems trite compared to what they did when they arrived places. There is healing in honest remembering and laughing or forgiving the weaknesses of those no longer with us.

Continually recognizing that our memories can only be about the past will assist us in "putting loved ones in a new place." Our memories of them are very present to us, but they themselves are no longer physically present, no matter how hard we wish it. When we "place them in the past" that doesn't mean we forget them. It means we take time to accept the reality of their departure from our present world, working through the pain of grief, and adjusting to a world without our loved one. We can remember them without being haunted by them.

As stated at the beginning, grief does not naturally or automatically lead to growth. There are many lives stalled, broken, and distorted by grief. God's help in facing and dealing with a loss is one of the essential resources in growing through grief. As with exercise and physical development in a world of pain, growth does not come pain-free. As C.S. Lewis in The Problem of Pain, so beautifully expressed it, "pain is God's megaphone" He gets our attention through it and His purpose is that we grow and mature through life to become like the perfect man Christ Jesus. Like Him, we will also be acquainted with grief on our journey through life (see Isaiah 53:3); like Him we can grow through grief.

Personal Growth and Discussion Questions:

1. Shortly after your loved one died could you close your eyes and imagine in your mind what they looked like? And then over time the image fades. Yes or No

2. When you close your eyes what can you still see and what do you remember most?

3. What was your loved one's voice like? Describe it.

4. Can you imagine them walking, sleeping, laughing, crying, talking, and thinking?

5. Which memory still causes you the most pain?

6. What memory gives you the most comfort?

Grief Resources

Growing Through Grief

DrTom Morris

ISBN 978-0-557-16247-5

GrowThroughGrief.com

GrievingTeens.com

Search iTunes for "grief"

MEETINGSPICE.COM

Youth Worker Materials can be found by searching for

"meeting spice" on iTunes

GrievingTeens Publishing

ISBN 978-0-557-16247-

ISBN 978-0-557-17095-1

ISBN 978-0-557-17043-2

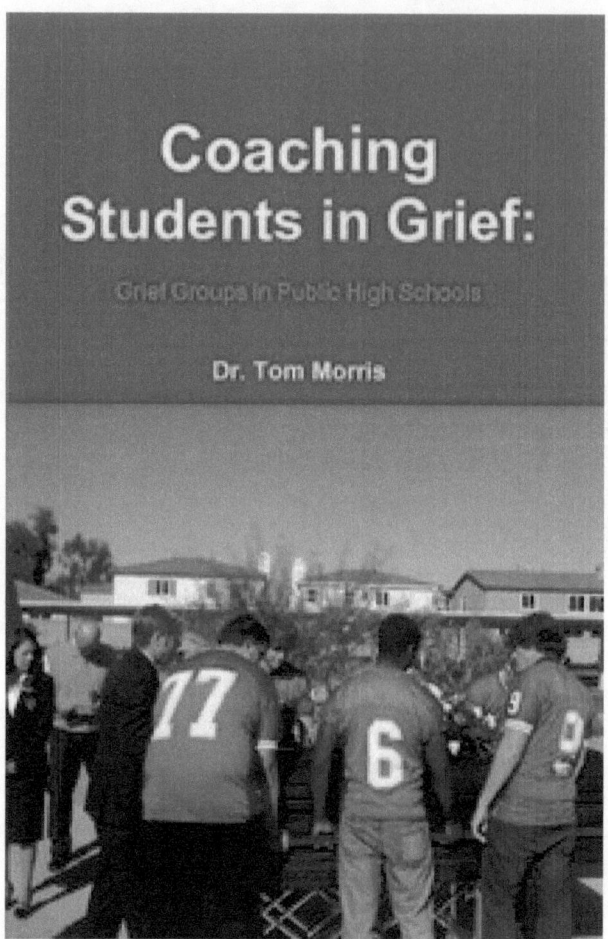

Coaching
Students in Grief:

Grief Groups in Public High Schools

Dr. Tom Morris

Making Sense
Out of Death
A Grief Devotional

Dr. Tom Morris
Author of Growing Through Grief

About the Author

Dr. Tom Morris

Tom has been married and worked with YFC for 35 years.
He has worked in Chicago, LA, Korea, and in the Desert with young people.
Tom's wife Audrey is a college Professor. Tom and Audrey have three children William is 27 and working on his Masters at Azusa Pacific University. Katherine 24 is a high school graduate and works full-time. Caroline is 20 an a Junior at APU.

Education:
Trinity Evangelical Divinity School, DMN 12/04
Student at Simon Greenleaf School of Law 1982-86 (Apologetics)
M Div. TEDS 1978 (World Evangelism/Missions and Youth)
SUNY at Buffalo BA Speech Communication/ Christianity 1975

Dr. Tom Morris is available to speak to your group. He can speak on Death, Dying and Grief Issues as well as other topics on the Bible, C.S. Lewis.